Portville Free Library
Portville, New York 14770

ARCHERY
is for me

ARCHERY
is for me

text and photographs by
Art Thomas

 Lerner Publications Company   Minneapolis

The author wishes to thank Robbie Swanson and Jackie Suk and their families for their time and talent. The author also thanks The National Field Archery Association and the members of the Parma Archery Club and C. F. Carrol for their help.

To R. Swanson and everyone else who is active in promoting archery as a sport

LIBRARY OF CONGRESS CATALOGING IN PUBLICATION DATA

Thomas, Art, 1952-
  Archery is for me.

  (The Sports for me books)
  SUMMARY: A young archer explains how to hold a bow properly, how to aim and shoot, and how to maintain and repair equipment.

  1. Archery—Juvenile literature. [1. Archery] I. Title. II. Series: Sports for me books.

  GV1189.T48   799.3'2   81-22
  ISBN 0-8225-1091-X   AACR1

Copyright © 1981 by Lerner Publications Company

All rights reserved. International copyright secured. No part of this book may be reproduced in any form whatsoever without permission in writing from the publisher except for the inclusion of brief quotations in an acknowledged review.

Manufactured in the United States of America

International Standard Book Number: 0-8225-1091-X
Library of Congress Catalog Card Number: 81-22

Hello! My name is Robbie. My favorite sport is archery. Archery is shooting with a bow and arrow. It's really a great sport. I first became interested in archery because every day on the way to school I passed a shooting range.

One Saturday I saw my friend Jackie practicing there. So I asked her about the sport. Jackie told me that archery was great if you like the out of doors. She said it also takes a lot of skill and practice.

I signed up for lessons at our neighborhood recreation center, and I often practiced with Jackie. I've been shooting for almost a year now, and I've really learned a lot about archery! Let me tell you about some of the things I've learned.

Archery is a very old sport. Bows and arrows from long ago have been found in almost every part of the world. Ancient cave drawings show that people used bows and arrows for hunting. People then had to hunt for food in order to survive.

Today some people still use bows for hunting. But most **archers**, like the members of the archery club Jackie and I belong to, shoot at targets instead. Shooting at targets takes skill and strength. That's what makes archery such a terrific sport.

This is one kind of arrow I use for shooting at targets. The steel tip of the arrow is called the **point**. The point screws on to the **shaft**, or long part, of the arrow. Aluminum shafts are the most popular today, but some are made from wood, fiberglass, stainless steel, or graphite.

Shafts sometimes have colored bands on them. These bands are called **crests**. Crests help archers identify which arrows are theirs.

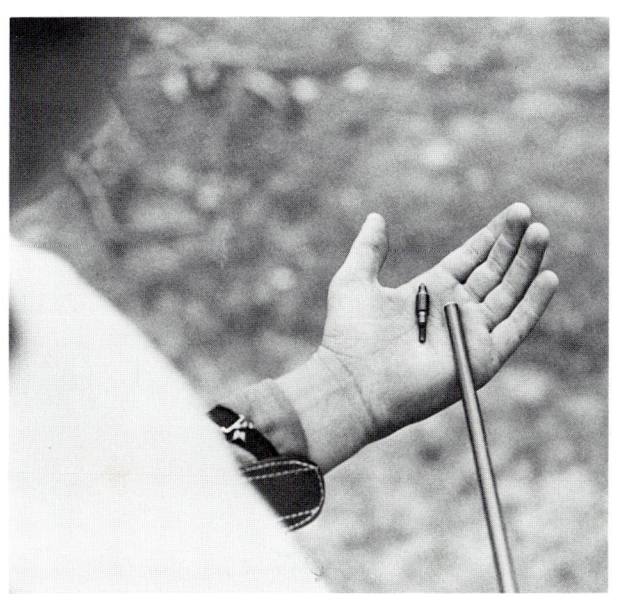 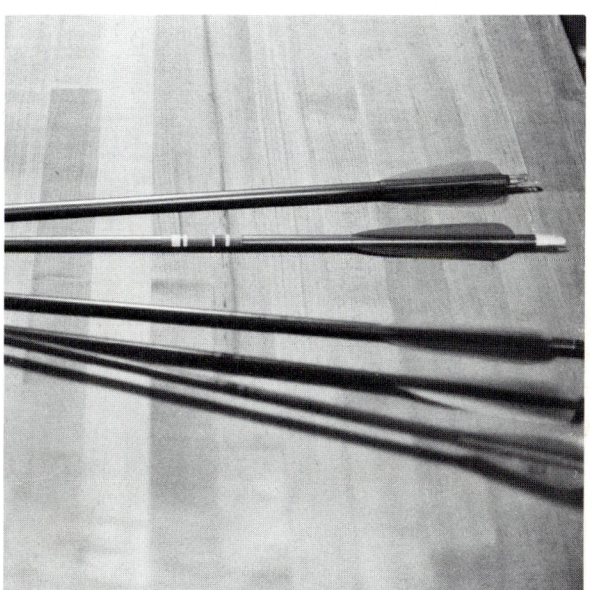

The back part of the shaft holds the **vanes**, or **fletching**. These are the feathers found on most arrows. Vanes used to be made from turkey feathers. Today arrows usually have plastic vanes.

At the very end of the arrow is a **nock**. A nock is a small notch that prevents the arrow from slipping off the bowstring.

Arrows come in different lengths. I use a 28-inch (70 cm) arrow. The length of the arrow depends on the length of the archer's arms and on the kind of bow that is used.

I was really excited when I got my own bow for a birthday present. I have a **recurve** bow. It is named for the backward bend in the bow. In a recurve bow, the string touches the bow for several inches at each end. Learning to use the recurve bow was a real challenge for me. But Jackie was nice about answering my questions and helping me.

One of the first archery skills I learned was how to **brace** the bow, or how to put the bowstring in place. The easiest way to brace the bow is called **push-pull bracing**.

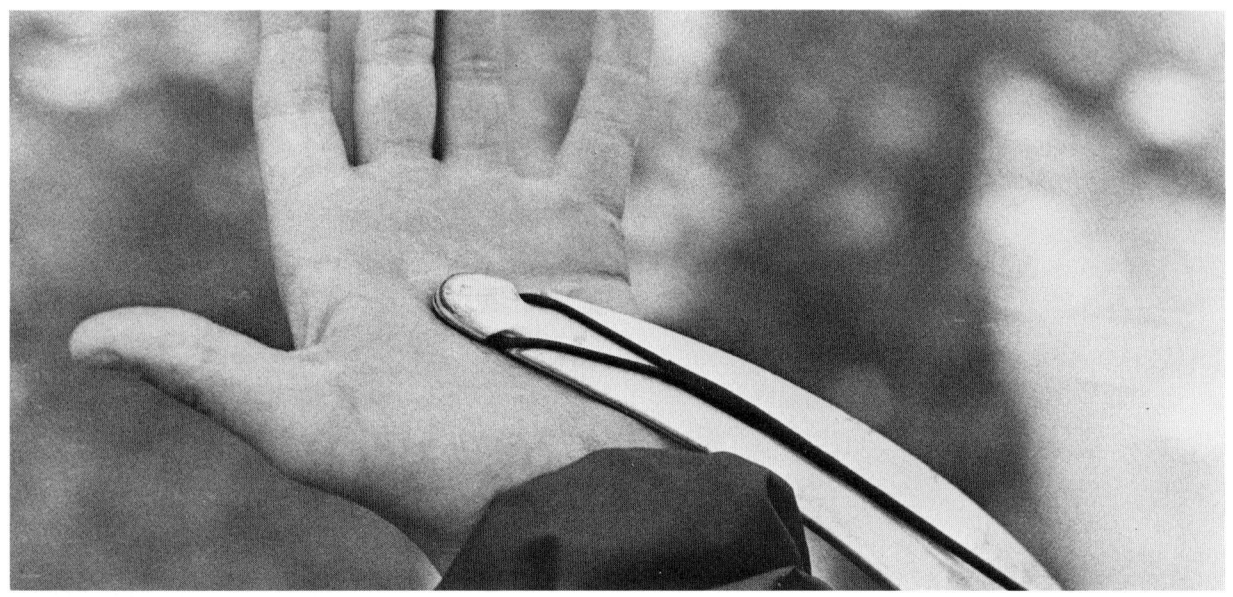

First you put one end of the string in the notch at the lower end of the bow. The wooden ends of the bow are called **limbs**.

Then, with the string in place, set the lower limb by the instep of your foot. But do not step on the bow. Your foot will just hold the bow steady.

Now pull in on the center of the bow. At the same time, use your other hand to push the upper limb down. I discovered this is not easy because the bow is stiff and hard to bend. I really had to use my muscle! Then, using your thumb and first finger, slip the string onto the upper notch of the bow.

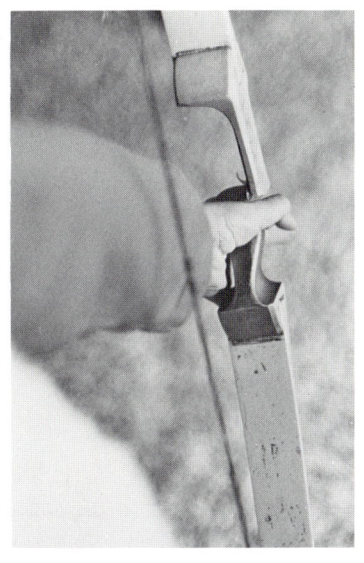

After the bow is braced, it is ready for shooting. Shooting is a difficult skill to master. Every small step, from gripping the bow to releasing the string, must be done right. I grip my bow as if I were shaking hands with it. A proper grip is important. It helps to prevent the bow from moving when I'm shooting.

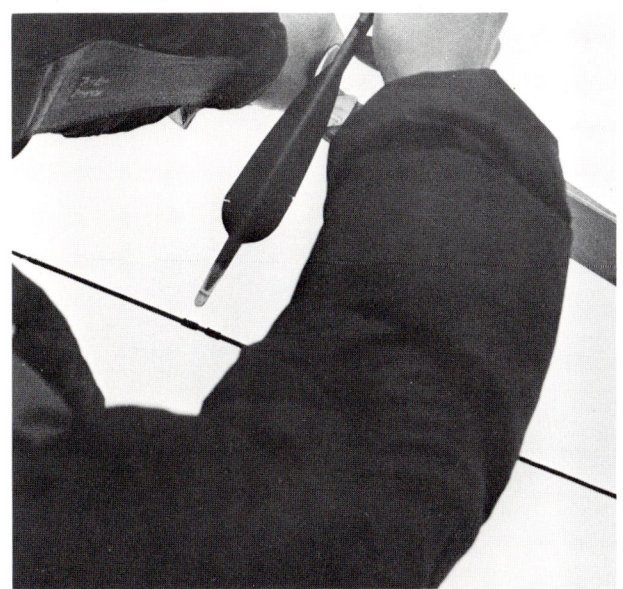
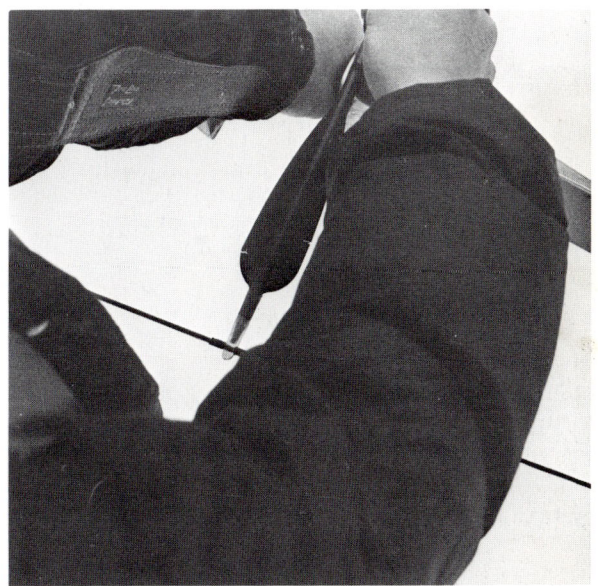

Next I select an arrow from my **quiver**. A quiver is a special case for holding arrows. Then I put the arrow on the bowstring. The string slips into the notch at the back of the arrow. This is called **nocking**. You should always nock the arrow at the same place on the bowstring. You can use metal clips or other marks on the string to show where the **nocking point** is.

I learned to point my bow down and slightly away from my body when nocking the arrow. If I were to accidently release the arrow from this position, it would hit the ground instead of another person. If you do not follow safety rules in archery, you should not be on a shooting range. Your carelessness could injure another archer.

The next step is grasping the string. I grasp the string with my first three fingers. The string rests in the groove where my fingers bend, and my first finger is just above the arrow. My second and third fingers are below the arrow. I curl my thumb and little finger toward my palm to get them out of the way.

Now I am ready to **draw**. Drawing is pulling the string back with the arrow on it. I begin by bringing the bow up. My bow arm is extended at shoulder height. As I draw the string back with my right hand, I keep my head turned toward the target.

The arrow should slide back smoothly on a little ledge called the **arrow rest**. At first my arrow always slid off of the arrow rest. This happened because I was holding my arrow too tightly. But with lots of practice, I corrected this problem.

I always finish my draw at an **anchor point** near the corner of my mouth. Having an anchor point helps to make my draw the same each time. And I can correct my aim more easily. I aim by looking down the shaft of the arrow toward my target. When the bowstring is drawn, the point should extend about two inches (5 cm) beyond the bow.

I aim my first arrow at the center of the target. This may not be the best place to aim. But after shooting several arrows and seeing where they have landed, I can correct my aim. I may have to aim higher or lower in order to hit the center of the target. This is because my height, the length of the arrow, and the strength of my bow all affect the arrow's flight.

The **release** is the real moment of truth in archery! On the release, you relax your fingers and let go of the bowstring. Your hands and arms should remain still and not jerk. It is especially important not to move your drawing hand forward.

 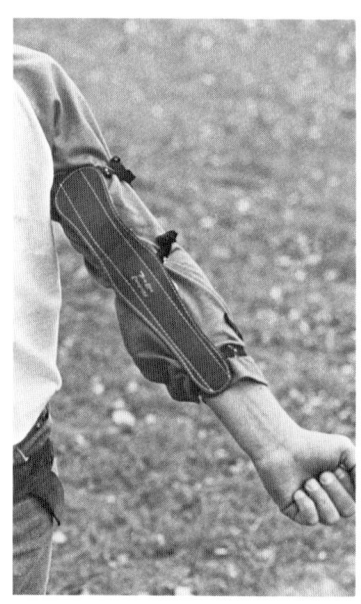

When I shoot, I strap an **arm guard** to my bow arm. An arm guard is made from leather or plastic, and it protects my arm from injury as the released string snaps back. I also wear a **finger tab**. This is a piece of leather that protects my fingers where they come into contact with the bowstring. Some archers prefer a shooting glove instead.

Practice is really important in archery. I often practice at the **shooting range**. Shooting ranges are special open areas set up for target shooting. There the targets are placed from 20 to 80 yards (18 to 72 m) away.

I shoot at targets from a **shooting line** that is marked with chalk or with stones in the ground. Arrows are shot in groups called **ends**. In the sport of target archery, an end has six arrows.

If you are shooting with other people, you cannot cross the shooting line until everyone has shot their end.

I learned that the rule about not crossing the shooting line is so strict that even if you drop an arrow, you cannot step over the line to pick it up. But you are allowed to pull the arrow in by reaching with your bow.

Collecting the arrows after you have shot an end is called **retrieving**. Arrows that have hit the target are pulled out carefully so that the points will not break. Before pulling the arrow out with one hand, you should always put the other hand on the target near the arrow.

If an arrow has gone so deeply into the target that the vanes are stuck, the arrow must be pulled through from the back of the target. But this may damage the fletching. You must also be careful when retrieving the arrows that are stuck in the ground. Always brush the dirt off before shooting the arrows again.

I like keeping records of my target shooting to see how I'm improving. Records are kept on a point system, and you get points every time you hit the target. An arrow that is close to the center of the target is worth more points than one nearer to the edge of the target. It's really exciting when I hit the center!

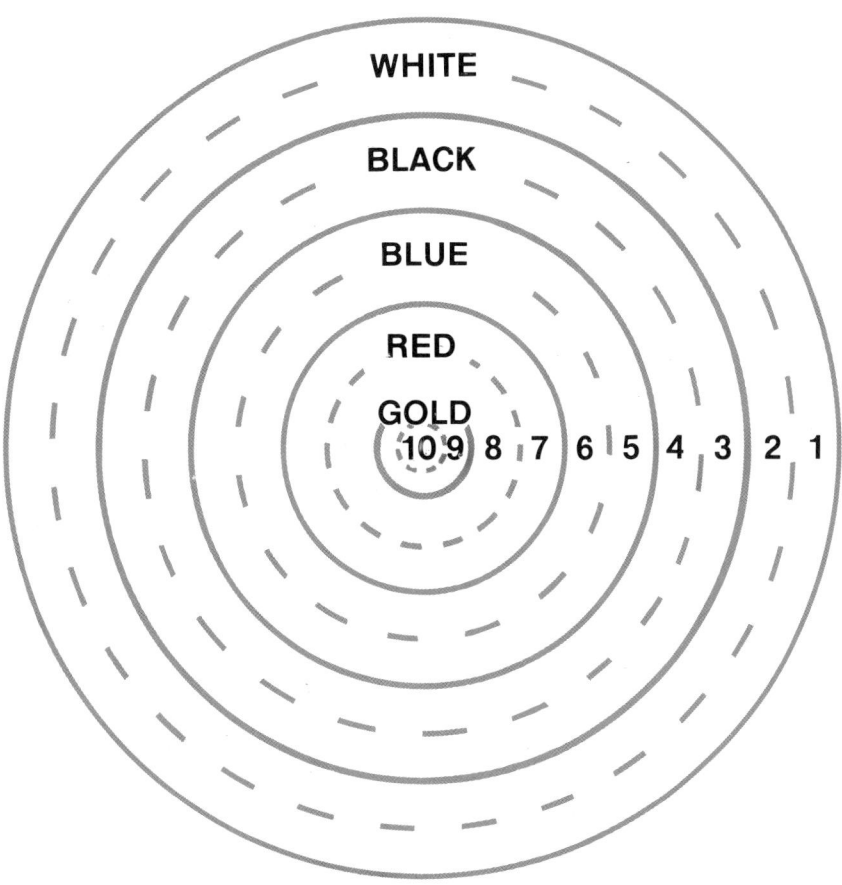

A target looks like this. It has five colored circles. Each colored area is divided into two parts. The center circles are gold. You are awarded 10 or 9 points for each arrow that lands there. The red circles count 8 and 7 points. The blue circles are worth 6 and 5 points. The black circles count 4 and 3 points. The outside white circles are worth 2 points or 1 point. You are given the higher point if your arrow lands on a dividing line.

Even though target archery is fun, I like field archery even better. In field archery we shoot on **field courses**. They're really neat because they trail through the woods.

Once you start out on a field course, you must always walk forward through it or exit on special paths. Never go back the way you came in. Backtracking is dangerous because you might get hit by other archers who are shooting.

A field course has 14 targets. The targets are at different distances from the archers. They are set from 7 to 80 yards (6 to 72 m) away. And the targets are different sizes depending on how far away they are. They can range from 6 to 24 inches (15 to 60 cm) across. We shoot from behind wooden stakes in the ground. Stakes for kids are closer to the targets than the stakes for adults.

Real hunting is not allowed at our club's field course because our members believe that wildlife protection is very important. But the field course is designed to match some of the conditions that a real hunter might find. Often the targets are pictures of animals.

In a field archery animal round, an end has three arrows. Each arrow must be numbered. If your first arrow hits the target, you are awarded more points than if your second or third arrow hits the target. This is because the first arrow is always the most important to a real hunter.

The animal targets have areas of different point values. The small area is called the **vital area**. The bigger area is called the **wound area**. You get more points if your arrow lands in the vital area. Here is a chart of the scores:

ARROW	AREA	POINTS
First	Vital	20
First	Wound	16
Second	Vital	14
Second	Wound	10
Third	Vital	8
Third	Wound	4

Sometimes **circle** targets are used on field courses, too. There are two types of circle targets—the **field** target and the **hunter** target.

The field target has a black center, a white middle ring, and a black outer ring.

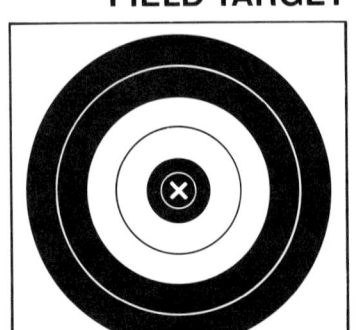
FIELD TARGET

The hunter target has a white center and a black outer ring. A fine white line divides the black ring into two scoring areas. On both hunter and field targets, the center is worth five points. The middle ring is worth four points, and the outer circle is worth three points.

HUNTER TARGET

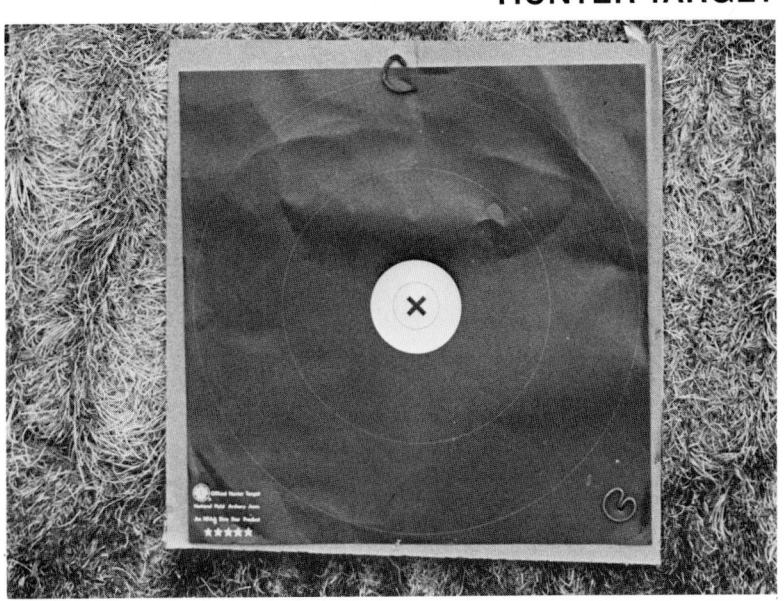

In both field and hunter rounds, four arrows make an end. We shoot in groups of four to six people, and everyone helps count the points for scoring.

After I learned all these things about archery, I entered a tournament with Jackie. Jackie scored more points than I did, but we both had fun. I know I'll do better after more practice. And Jackie had a mechanical advantage over me because of the kind of bow she uses.

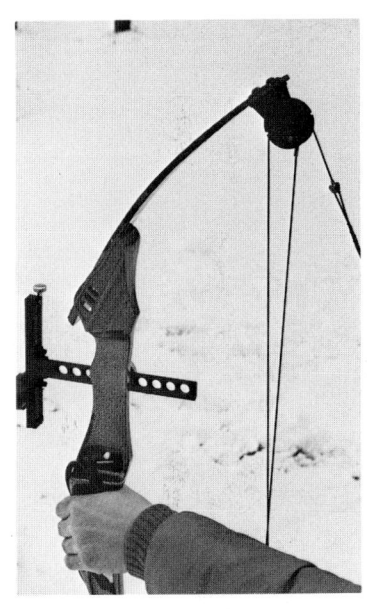

Jackie uses a **compound bow**. On a compound bow, the bowstring is attached through wheels on each end. The wheels help to lower the amount of energy you need to draw the string back. So when you draw, it is easy to hold the string at the anchor point until you are ready for the release.

Arrows shot from a compound bow usually travel faster and more accurately than arrows that are shot from a recurve bow. And Jackie has another piece of equipment that helps her to improve her accuracy even more. It is a **bowsight**.

The bowsight is attached to Jackie's bow. Jackie looks through the tiny hole on the bowsight and aims directly at the target. Before she shoots, she has to adjust the settings for her distance from the target. This is more accurate than using an aiming point like I do.

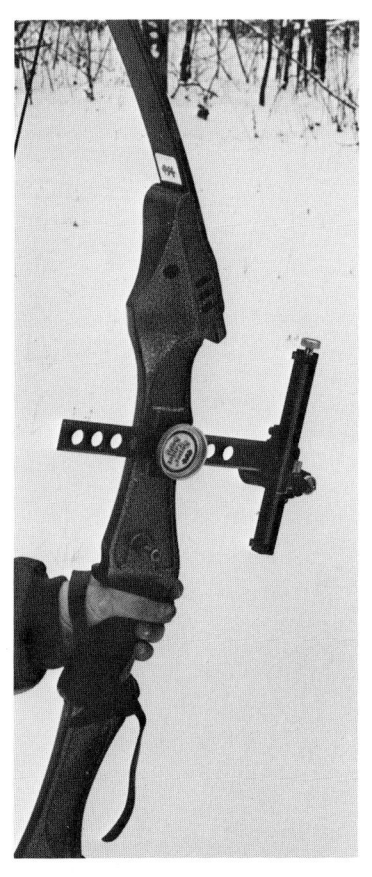

Another piece of archery equipment is a **stabilizer**. A stabilizer is a metal rod with a weight at the end. It screws into the back of the bow and extends in front of the archer. The stabilizer helps to keep the bow steady, and it prevents a "kick," or jerk, when the bowstring is released.

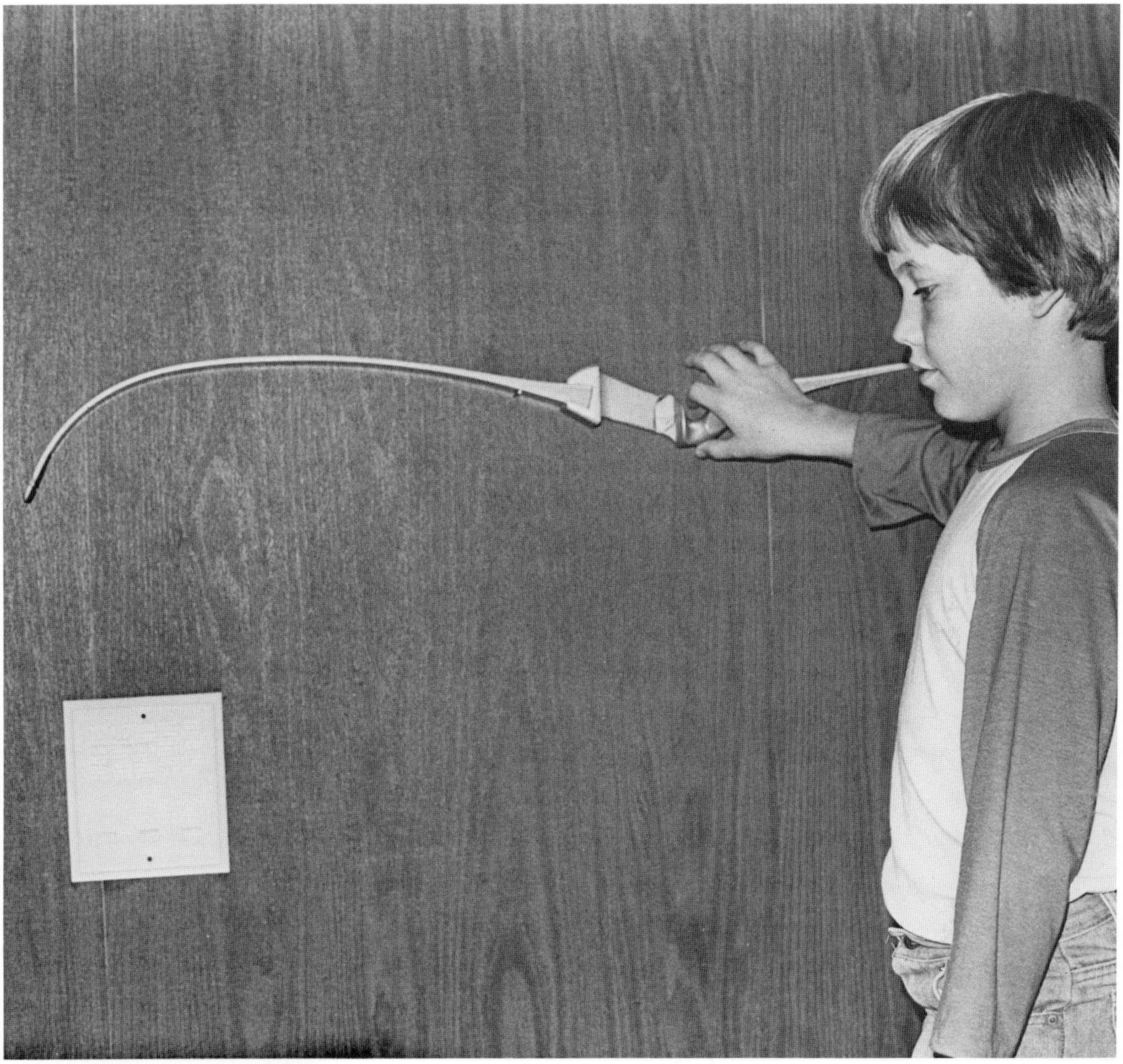

I also learned that it is important to take good care of your archery equipment. A recurve bow should never be stored in a braced position. To keep the limbs from warping, you should hang it like this, away from the heat. And remember to rub your bowstring with beeswax once a week to keep it in good condition.

I'm careful with my arrows, too, sometimes they get bent. So I've learned how to repair them by hand. My archery club also has a special tool to straighten arrows.

I know how to repair damaged fletching, too. This is done with a **fletching jig**. I put a special glue on the edge of the vane, attach it to the jig, and wait for it to dry. It feels good to be able to do these repairs myself. And I save money, too.

Our archery club can shoot all year long. During the winter we have lots of snow where I live, so it is often cold when we shoot. But I like the changing scenery on our field course. And no matter what season it is, I know that archery is for me!

Words about ARCHERY

ANCHOR POINT: The position of your drawing hand when aiming the arrow

ARCHER: A person who shoots with a bow and arrow

ARM GUARD: A piece of leather or plastic that protects your bow arm from the released bowstring

BACK: The side of the bow away from the string

BOWNOCK: The notch at the end of an arrow where the string is held

BOWSIGHT: A device attached to the bow that is used for aiming

BRACE: To prepare a bow for shooting; to put the string in the notches of the bow

COMPOUND BOW: A bow with a mechanical device to make drawing easier

CREST: The colored markings on the shaft of the arrow used for identification

DRAW: To pull the bowstring back

END: A group of arrows shot before retrieving

FACE: The side of the bow facing the string

FINGER TAB: A piece of leather used to protect the fingers where they come in contact with the bow

FLETCHING: The feathers on an arrow

HANDLE: The center part of the bow that an archer grips

LIMBS: The wooden ends of a bow

NOCK: The notch at the end of an arrow that prevents the arrow from slipping off the bowstring

NOCKING: Putting the arrow on the bowstring

POINT: The metal tip of an arrow

QUIVER: A case for holding arrows

RANGE: A target shooting area; the distance you shoot

RECURVE BOW: A type of bow named for its backward bend

RELEASE: To slip your fingers off the bowstring and send the arrow to the target

RETRIEVE: To collect the arrows after the entire end has been shot

SHAFT: The long part of the arrow

TAB: A piece of protective leather worn on the fingers that hold the string

STABILIZER: A weighted rod that absorbs shock when shooting and prevents the bow from moving

VANE: *See* Fletching

ABOUT THE AUTHOR/PHOTOGRAPHER

ART THOMAS is active in sports as an instructor, a participant, and a fan. As a drama and composition teacher in Cleveland, Ohio, Mr. Thomas is also involved with professional and community theater, both as an actor and a director. In addition, he writes travel and feature articles for newspapers and magazines and has authored other books in the *Sports for Me* series.

```
J 799 .32 T 4-6
Thomas, Art, 1952-
   Archery is for me
```

DATE DUE		
	DISCARDED FROM THE	
	PORTVILLE FREE LIBRARY	

PORTVILLE FREE LIBRARY

PORTVILLE, N. Y.

Member Of
Chautauqua-Cattaraugus Library System